A Dance of Black and White

Mariano Duque

Disclaimer

This is a work of complete fiction. Names of characters, places, dialogues, ideas, and incidents are either the product of the author's imagination or are used fictitiously.

About the Author

Mariano Duque was born in Guatemala and came to the United States when he was nine. He migrated with his family to find a treatment for his young brother's illness and hopefully a cure. Mariano has always been known to have an appetite for Literature, often going through a new book in a couple of days. He grew up in Los Angeles and was always exposed to different backgrounds and people.

He discovered his love for storytelling and writing at a young age when he would awe his friends with his ability to express stories and his ever-expanding imagination. He graduated from California State University in Los Angeles shortly after the COVID-19 pandemic ended. Now, he is working to help kids embrace a love for reading and the English language as his teachers did when he was growing up.

When Mariano first came to the United States and was enrolled in school, one of his teachers gifted him a book, and along with that book came the hope that one day he would master English as a second language.

Mariano has always been inspired by reading the works of writers such as Paulo Cohelo, Don Miguel Ruiz, and Dan Brown.

Page Left Blank Intentionally

Chapter 1: A New Beginning

There she was now, Jenny, a girl of no less than 5'4", standing in the mirror. The room was big enough for ten people, yet only a king-size bed was placed in the center of the room against the wall. The bed had two sets of pillows that matched the bed sheets. They were a carmine red and had a gold bed frame that took the shape of wings. Next to the bed on both sides, there were two tables of a dark brown type of wood that didn't reflect light but, were each with a small lamp that stood on top and could be moved for reading. One of the tables had a small black book similar to a bible with a vast cross that was the cover of the book and wrapped in a black onyx or ivory colored chain that had a cross with gold outlines on it.

The book had golden pages and couldn't be read. The pages were empty, but the book looked as new as if it had been bought recently. In front of the bed against the other wall, a giant 100-inch plasma screen was placed on the wall and had channel 11 on, and the 11 o'clock news was on, but the TV was on mute. The room was a gentle dark red color that matched the bed sheets. These spaces in the room's corners gave an elegant and luxurious look.

A mirror was on the side of the bed, and a girl observed her reflection. Her once light brown hair was now black and reflected no light. Her dark brown eyes looked lifeless like she had nothing to live for anymore. She got dressed in her work outfit but instead considered wearing a pair of black ripped jeans that were thin enough to be considered skinny jeans, except that the material was much more comfortable. Instead of her usual white boots, she opted for a pair of white sneakers. Ideally, the boots were meant to make her look about his height when standing next to him. She decided to take the patrol easier tonight and changed into a long-sleeved white top. Usually, she would wear her white overcoat that reached a little below her knees, but this time, she wore a long black overcoat made of a material similar to leather. As she put it on, her body felt heavier. She was never accustomed to the weight of it. She wondered how he could possibly run and move with something so heavy. She then went to the table near the king-size bed and got her cell phone, which was also white. From the string that was attached to it, she picked up the black chain that was wrapped around the black book. Then, she tucked the black book into the overcoat's inside pocket. Then, she walked out of the room through the window, staring into the crescent moon. She jumped off and landed on top of another roof. She then kept jumping from roof to roof, looking above her head and heading towards a house that appeared to be a five-story hospital yet looked like a plain old building. She walked into the front door where she was greeted by another girl. She was a redhead who was an inch less than her and wore a uniform like hers but had a combination of white and faded red.

She asked, "Are you sure you want to keep working even after what happened about a year ago?"

The brunette just looked at her and said, "That's what he would have wanted, right? Wasn't it his last wish for us to make sure the mistakes of the past don't repeat themselves?"

"Yes, I know his wishes. We were all there when he told you, but aren't you working yourself too hard? I mean, your work has become a lot harder since his death. But still, it's ironic, you know," the redhead said.

"What's ironic?" Jenny asked.

"Well, before, you used to tell him to give himself some time to rest since he was almost always working on some project he didn't want anyone to know about," the redhead responded.

"I remember now. Yes, he always used to work himself to the point of exhaustion, which always surprised me since he still carried on with his job and human life without ever revealing the truth," Jenny paused for a while and then continued. "It's odd. You know how he and I met, and after so long, it didn't last."

The redhead listens and looks at the other girl with a sad expression that says that she is more affected by his death than she is.

"Hey, why don't we stop talking about him? You know it's unhealthy for you to talk about him so soon. You know how you get when you let yourself go that much," the redhead finally said.

"Yeah, I know I'm still taking antidepressants. Honestly, he was the one person I never expected to give himself up like that. I wonder if the truth behind why he did it was that it was a way for him to be free from me or because he cared about these humans," Jenny responded.

"I could never figure him out," the redhead said. "Even when we went out, he kept others out of his head."

"Yeah, I still can't believe he's gone. Everything has no meaning anymore, almost like something is missing," Jenny said. "You know it's weird, but sometimes I feel he's still alive but hiding somewhere, hoping I forget and move on."

"Don't talk like that. You know he loved you more than he loved his freedom. Hey, and remember, if he had wanted to leave, he would have left you a long time ago and gone with someone else or to another country like France," the redhead said. "You know he loved that country. He always talked about the time you followed him there when he made you stay home while he took care of business."

"It's odd, though. Despite his being gone, some remnants are still around, like a sword he used to use. I thought when one disappears, all items disappear, too," Jenny responded.

"You know it takes a while for energy to disappear entirely, and according to how much power he had, it may even take centuries before it's all gone. He is still weaker than my boyfriend, though," the redhead said, snickering a little.

Jenny rolled her eyes in annoyance and said, "You never change a year after his death, and you still mock him about how your boyfriend outranked him."

"I'm just being truthful, gone and all, but he was always weaker, and it's odd how only he could win. I don't understand if his death was worth the win," the redhead said.

Jenny was not visibly frustrated and annoyed. "Of course it was! Everything is back to normal."

"Sorry, I got carried away. It's hard for me to get used to this since… I mean… I can't say anything without hurting your feelings anymore," the redhead responded. "You have become so sensitive I can't say anything without triggering you."

"It's okay. You know, he always told me that I should always try to train and face my problems on my own since he said he wouldn't always be around, and now I know what he meant," Jenny said. "Everything is so complicated that I can't walk into class without thinking the reason he's not in here with us is because he got ill, or if he died, or if he's running in late, like how he did because he overslept."

"Yeah, it's fantastic, though, about the number of people who came to his funeral," the redhead responded. "People from all over the globe were helped by someone he helped, and so on."

"Yeah, it's odd since he used to say he disliked humans and pitied them. I don't understand," Jenny responded.

"Understand what?" the redhead asked.

"He told me once I was at a higher rank than him, I could finally read what was opened in his book," Jenny replied.

"Hey, what do you mean by finally reading his book?" the redhead got confused.

"Sorry, it's nothing. I just felt like he was here for some reason," Jenny said.

"I told you to stop thinking of him! It's unhealthy for you," the redhead replied.

"I know, but…" Jenny couldn't complete her sentence.

"Don't but me," the redhead sighed. "I'll tell you what William and I will take over tonight. While you go home, lay in bed and try to think about something that is not him."

"I wish I could, but you know me. I have to do something, or else I'll start to get lonely or depressed," Jenny responded.

Suddenly, an elevator door opens, and a boy of no less than 18 comes into the room, kisses the redhead, and whispers something in her ear.

"Okay, I got it. I'll go ahead and wait for you until you're done here," the redhead said after the boy finished murmuring.

"What's going on?" Jenny asked.

"Well, you know I'm not good at breaking news to people, and you know he always took it upon himself to deliver bad news. I know you and him had the policy of not killing the messenger, so…" the boy said.

Jenny got annoyed. "So, what? I know he's gone, but that doesn't mean I can't hope he fell somewhere due to the shock wave! Remember, you convinced me he wouldn't die so quickly, even in his weakened state."

"I know what I said! It's just that it's been a year, and I haven't found any traces of him. You know what this means, right?" the boy snapped back.

"No! I don't believe this - you are lying! You're supposed to be able to track anyone, dead or alive, no matter where they are, and you are telling me that the great Sir William can't find my long-lost boyfriend?" Jenny replied, clearly frustrated.

"Hold it. Listen, I know what I said, and I'm sorry for raising your hopes. That's not important. What's important is making sure it doesn't awaken again," William said.

"How could that thing still be alive? He killed it. I saw it become dust and vanish," Jenny replied.

"I know that, but the council says that it still lives, and it may awaken again soon. All he did was seal it away, but the seal is getting weaker, and we can't duplicate a seal that powerful," William tried to reason.

"How about the council? Aren't they supposed to be at the highest ranks possible and were supposed to be unbeatable?" Jenny responded.

"You got it. I was one of them, and I outranked them, and even then, I could not recreate the seal or even damage it," William said.

"Now I know he's missing," Jenny said with conviction. "You're admitting this is insane, and you're alleged to be stronger, smarter, and faster than him."

"I am, but somehow, I feel weaker now. It's like it's a dream," William responded.

"But it's not. Sadly, I wish I could bring him back. Maybe then he would take charge and calm us down," Jenny said.

"Calm US down? Do you mean calm YOU down?" William asked. "You're the one who wants him back. We all miss him, but we know he wants us to move on, and that's what we are doing while you keep trying to find him even though he's dead."

It took hours until the brunette and William stopped talking, got on the elevator, and reached the 5th floor. They both stepped out of the elevator and walked into an office with a brown carpet and pictures of paintings done by Picasso and other famous Renaissance painters. A laptop on a desk was opened, facing the window, which directly showed the moon. William walked up to his desk, sat down, and typed his password to access his files. He then looked at the brunette and, with astonishment, made her come next to him and showed her something that gave her a slight sense of hope and broke her heart to shreds.

"I can't believe this…" William said.

"I don't get it. Why are we still between the archer and the Arachne?" Jenny asked.

"It might have to do with the beast," William responded.

"But he killed it. I saw it!" Jenny alleged.

"Yes but if you know, we are right in the middle, and mercury is glowing stronger than it had when he killed it. So this means that maybe he's still alive, but if I can't find traces of him, then it means he might as well be, you know…" William stopped speaking.

"Well, what should I do then?" Jenny questioned.

"Go home and rest. I'll message you if anything comes up," William reassured her.

"Okay, but promise me you will…" Jenny pleaded.

"I will!" William said.

Jenny is awaited by Rose, who is patiently tapping her feet, waiting for the other two to finish. Rose questions Jenny about taking so long and how she needs to rest. Jenny looks down to the floor, about to apologize, but Rose stops her and nags her about being too apologetic. "You have to stop being so soft. Show some backbone, at least!"

Jenny apologizes, only for Rose to almost hit her on the head with her first. The girls head over to Jenny's and Rose finds how a mess her room is.

"How can you be living in this mess? This is so unlike you!" Picking up the scattered articles of clothing, she teases Jenny that Daemon must have left her after noticing what a slob she had become recently. Jenny giggles a bit, showing a bit of her old self, but immediately falls back into her saddened state. After talking for a couple of hours, the girls say their goodbyes, and Rose exits the building, leaving Jenny alone, hoping things will be better for her the next day.

After Rose left, Jenny tried to go to sleep, but her mind kept tormenting her about what Wallace had told her. *It is evident they don't care,* she thought to herself. *It's clear they never cared for me, nor did they even want to tell me the truth about my 'missing' partner. All they care about is themselves.*

Jenny got out of bed and reached into a cabinet full of medication, took the pills, and as she wished, she could just see him one last time. Suddenly, her world began to spin, and she slowly tried to reach the bed. As she finally managed to reach the foot of the bed, she collapsed and went into a deep sleep. All she could think about was that day, the argument they had, him coming back and fighting for her, and the last image that was burned into her subconscious was the eyes… those damn eyes that she feared so much.

Chapter 2: The Dream

Dawn had come. The birds chirped, and light entered the room. There she was, lying in her bed. Something about the dream she had last night made her feel uneasy, and now she wanted him back more than ever. She remembered how he always hugged her when she had nightmares and how he used to sweet-talk her to sleep.

She began to toss and turn in bed without the intention of getting up. She then heard a faint voice whisper her name.

"Jenny… Come, Jenny… Come and find me. I need you."

She then jumped out of bed and looked around. Suddenly, the room became dark, and the sun's light became dull and lifeless. Another voice, faint but audible, whispered,

"What can you do? Nothing, you're just an insect! Face it! Without him, you're nothing! You're weak that's why he left you! That's why he's with someone else. Give up. You'll never find him. He doesn't want to be found by anyone, especially you! Can't you see he left because you never faced your problems? Don't you know what

was going through his head? And yet you forced him to kill himself, and all for nothing. I'm still alive, and I'll devour you and your foolish friends."

She just cried and said, "No, you're wrong. He would never do that to me. I know him better than that. I knew what was going through his head. He was afraid, and he wanted to rest finally and never have to do what he did again."

She then began to shrug. She inched her body forward and slowly put her hands to her ears. She got on the floor and crouched down in a fetal position. With her hands to her ears, she closed her eyes and began to cry. Her body started shaking and feeling cold; the room became as cold as ice. Her breathing was a lot more difficult, and she felt pressure in her chest as if a rock was placed on her body, slowly crushing her and leaving her gasping for air. Suddenly, she felt the air blow as hard as a giant trumpet being played; the air was cold. She now knew where she was.

"I know where I am. I don't want to open my eyes. I know what's around me. I need him!"

Then she moved her hands slowly from her ears and

only heard the steady pace of the waves and could hear the birds singing. She then slowly got herself out of her fetal position and found the courage to open her eyes. She opened her eyes slowly, looking at the sky's white clouds. She wore a long white dress and felt a chill run down her spine. Then she looked toward her, and a long bridge surrounded it. The water was clear and blue, and you could see through it and see the fishes swimming - the colorful fishes of red, blue, yellow, and grey. She felt that chilling sensation persist more now. She looked at the bridge and decided to walk through it. She slowly moved, afraid of what she would find and what spoke to her. In her head, Jenny felt weak and afraid.

"I hope this isn't the same dream as before," she said. "I remember this bridge haunted him for some reason, but he never told me why."

She inched forward, a lot more confident, and pressed on, telling herself, "I am close. I'm halfway through. I can see the beach from here." She then found a crossroads facing towards where she saw the beach and the other misty, and nothing could be seen except the silhouette of a huge building.

She suddenly heard, "Jenny, Jenny, I need you. Please come. I need you, Jenny. I want you to cross the path covered in the mist." Now she knew where she was, and either way, she knew 'it' was close by. Suddenly, the ground began to shake, and the water moved more violently.

"Something big is coming," she said to herself.

Then, a large body moved next to her near the bridge, and all she saw was a long green tail. And then she knew what it was and where she was.

"No, this is a dream! He's not real! He can't harm me! He won't attack me." She then tightened her grip on the chain. The water now steered much harder, and the bridge collapsed behind her. She walked to where her lover's voice called, "Jenny, come, Jenny, I need you to come. Follow my voice."

She was in a trance and walked through the mist, and now she was in the middle of the sea, but the water was grayish and ash-like, and you could no longer see the fish. Then, out of the mist and below the water, several pillars made of stone rose, one after the other. These pillars were enormous. They seemed to reach the sky. Suddenly, a stone pyramid rose behind them in the center. Slowly, it rose out of the water, a shadow with giant red eyes that made her skin crawl; she knew what was before her.

She said to herself. "No, you can't be alive. He killed you. I saw it!"

"Foolish human. I can't be gotten rid of so quickly," the voice said.

"What do you want from me? Why do you keep attacking me?"

"It is not what I want but what my master wants," the voice said.

"Master?" Jenny asked confusingly.

"Since the beginning, we have both fought for control of the light and the darkness, yet light always seems to prevail, but not for long. We've been doing this since the beginning of civilization, and despite warnings, you humans never learn from mistake after mistake. That is why you must be destroyed!" the voice replied.

"But why us? What have we done to be treated with such hate?" Jenny asked.

"It's not what you have done. It's what others have

done. If humanity is let loose, I will continue to grow and become stronger. Soon, I'll be able to take to the skies, and then even he won't be able to stop me," the voice said.

"You're mistaken. He is still alive; he's going to come back and kill you once and for all," Jenny responded.

Suddenly, her vision became blurry, and then she saw a glimpse of what she didn't want to see. The sky became black, and darkness was all over her world until a glimmer of light broke through, and he took her away from it.

"Jenny, Jenny, wake up! I need you to wake up."

She opened her eyes and stood in her room, saying, "It was just a dream. I wish I knew what they mean, though."

She looked at the black book and tried to open it, and then the room lit up with a bright and intense white light. Now, she wasn't in her room.

"Where am I?" Jenny asked.

"Hey, it's been a while," the voice said.

"Who is this? Show yourself!" Jenny ordered.

"Sadly, you don't recognize my voice. Turn around. It's me," the voice responded.

Jenny turned around and saw a silhouette of a person with long hair and a pair of wings that reminded her of how he was before he died. The shadow stood there and said, "I am sorry for making you suffer like this."

"You don't have to apologize. You knew that either way, it would start to attack me anyway," Jenny said.

"I'm not ready to come back yet. I'm still weak, and I need time," the voice said.

"Why can't you come back?" Jenny asked.

"I'm beginning to weaken. For now, I can only keep him away from you, but…" the voice stopped. The shadow began to fade away slowly. It became dust, and before it completely vanished, it said, "Go to the tree and take my feather. Once you're there, just as the fruit gave the first humans knowledge, will it give you the ability to read my book and know how to stop what I started and what I should stop?"

Jenny wakes up in her room. William and the Rose surround her, and both look worried. They urge her that they'll all take a vacation, and then she might rest, but her eyes close, and all that comes out of her lips is, "I saw him. He's still alive."

"What on Earth are you talking about?" Rose asked.

"I saw him. He took me away from it," Jenny responded.

"Here you go again! What is wrong with you?" Rose said frustratingly.

"Jenny, enough of this nonsense! Do I have to suspend you further?" William said.

"But!-" Jenny began to speak, but Rose cut her off.

"Just give it a rest, please," Rose said.

"Listen, we will come to visit constantly. Just keep yourself out of trouble," William said.

Both exited the building, leaving behind Jenny. The young girl is left with her hair a mess, her room appearing as a hurricane had helped rearrange the once organized room into a disaster zone. Jenny gazes in disbelief that not only has her two closest friends turned their back on her, but she is on indefinite leave.

Rose turns back to look at Jenny and thinks to herself, *What's happening to you? Where is my friend, my colleague?*

Jenny keeps looking as they walk away, then she realizes she's holding a long black colored feather. She looks down at it in disbelief. *This wasn't a dream*, she thought to herself. She moves to her bed, pushes off the piles of books on the bed, and sits down to look at the little black book that belonged to her once lover. Suddenly, the voices return, tormenting the young girl. She suddenly remembers the eyes… those big, red eyes that just stared at her and seemed to only think of her as a meal.

Rose and William sit for dinner and begin to discuss the situation.

"Well, if you are going to cuss me off, just do it. I know I went too far," William began speaking.

"Too Far! You literarily told her that we, not just you but myself, didn't care about her well-being. I am disgusted, and you are sleeping outside tonight! No negotiations on this," Rose responded.

"Woman! It's my house. You cannot throw me out!" William protested.

"I just did!" she responded.

"Fine, I'll be back. Let me go talk to her," William said.

"Thank you!" Rose replied.

Chapter 3: Wishing

Inside a building, two people are sitting in a room with a giant-sized computer in the center against the wall. The computer is running a diagnosis and shows on the screen apparent causes, including fatigue, loss of appetite, and lack of sleep.

"It appears she didn't listen to what I told her," said a red-headed girl of 5'3", who looked worried. "She said, 'I saw him. He's still alive.' What could this mean?"

The red-headed girl ran another diagnosis on the computer, which read the same thing it had done before. "I don't understand why she was in such a bad state and those bruises on her arms and the look in her eyes; it's not normal. What could be happening first to him and now to Jenny? What could this mean? William, do you know?" the redhead questioned again.

"No, I don't understand what is happening either, and yet could it be what he warned me about all those years ago? But all I know is that we have not seen the last of that snake," William responded.

"But we can't just stand and not do anything. Just

look at Jenny; she would never hurt herself like this," Rose said.

"I know Jenny too, but remember, she's in denial. She still thinks Daemon is alive somewhere, and I'm afraid she will eventually find out and want me to take her to him," William replied.

"Well, is he alive or not?" Rose asked.

"He is dead... well, as far as I know...he's been dead for a year now. Remember, we were there and saw him vanish along with it. What's odd, though, is that one of his feathers is still around," William said.

"But, haven't you noticed that when we came into her room, we found her holding the feather in her hands and his book?" Rose questioned.

" Yeah, I know, and I took the feather," William retorted.

"But why?" Rose questioned again.

"I did it for her sake, and I'll oversee the book since it appears she can't even read it," William said.

"But, isn't she at a rank similar to Daemon then? Why can't she read it?" Rose probed.

"I guess she still isn't mature enough to read it," William guessed.

"What do you mean by not mature? She's more mature than me, and you put together.

"She has a weak mind. She still can't comprehend why he left the book for her care. She doesn't understand that the feather is a key and worst of all, she thinks and feels like he's still alive. Instead of training to get stronger mentally and physically, she worries about whether he will return," William said.

"But he's still alive, right?" Rose asked.

"NO!" William responded.

"Sshh! Speak more softly. You know she is here resting," Rose requested.

"Just shut up!" William responded angrily.

"Why did you start it?" Rose probed.

"Well, I'm ending it," William responded.

"You are acting like a child!" Rose said.

"And you're not!" William said sarcastically.

"Shut up, both of you!" they heard a voice from

behind. Both turn to see the bed and see a girl sitting down right up with her face red and full of tears. "Stop! Please stop arguing!"

"Jen… Jenny…I am sorry! I didn't mean to wake you up," Rose apologized profusely.

"Yeah, come on, you know us. We're always fighting for the nonsense that's no reason to cry, you know," William said.

"It's not you guys…" Jenny said.

They look at her, shocked by what they heard.

"It's not you guys, it's him," Jenny continued speaking. "I wish … No! I want him here. I want to go to him, so why won't he return? Doesn't he love me anymore? What did I do to drive him away?"

"Jenny, calm down…" the redhead said.

William sits beside her, facing away from her face, not to see how she is dressed and to avoid seeing her tearful eyes. He then begins to speak. "Listen, I know. I understand how much you love him, and I know how much you care for him. You two were so together that you shared even your days in the hospital. I remember that a few years ago, you got so wounded. He was so pissed off at me for not protecting you that he tried to fight me and burned me and then went after the demon that attacked you and killed it. But he was so careless that he got extremely wounded. Me and Rose here had to take him to the hospital. You two were in the same room next to each other for those two months. The funniest part was that he got a better fist, was more damaged than you, and didn't let anyone who wasn't him or a doctor come into the room."

"I remember that he stayed with me the rest of the two months in the same room and barely got out," Jenny responded. "Except only when he was asked to by a doctor. I remember him consoling me while I was sleeping. I know I didn't dream this, but I remember him saying that there was nothing he wouldn't do for me, and he promised me that no matter what, even if we were mad at each other, he would never hurt me or try to turn me away."

"We know that already," Rose said. "We videotaped him saying it and kept replaying it to him when you two would get into arguments."

"Yeah, he was always there," Jenny said with a sad look in her eyes. "And I can't believe I let him go like I did."

"The bet you two made on your relationships was stupid on your part," Rose and William said together.

"I know," Jenny admitted. "He asked me if I was sure to separate for three months."

"Well, he can't get away from his wife, can he?" William said, teasing Jenny.

"That's true," Jenny responded with a faded smile. "I forgot he and I have been married for a long time. I can't believe I forgot."

"I told you pretending to be a human gets to you after a while," William said.

"You weren't kidding. I forgot he and I had been married for centuries," Jenny responded.

"This is weird, though. We are all old, but we look like 16 to 17-year-olds even though we are either reborn or don't die," Rose said.

"That's true, but his family worries me," Jenny expressed. "His grandfather is his great-grandfather, yet they had to fight one another for the power of their blood right."

"You know he's not the original, right?" William asked.

"Why don't you just shut up? At least his techniques are all his own," Jenny said. "It's not his fault. Your people first thought of his techniques and never kept them within their circle."

"How about we change the subject?" William suggested. "Well, Jenny, tell us what happened to you. Why did you end up all scratched up as you did?"

"All I remember is hearing his and a foul voice. Then, I saw the temple and the snake he used to dream about, and everything was exactly like his, but he saved me while in his dreams. He was either attacked by it or woke up," Jenny replied.

"Are you sure you didn't dream it?" William questioned.

"I'm sure everything was as clear and vivid as I see you two," Jenny answered.

"It was just a dream, Jen. He was never there. Get it

through your thick skull. He's dead!" William said.

"Then, why did I see him? Why do I keep feeling like he's around, like he's still alive? Why shouldn't I search for him? Tell me the truth, is he dead or alive?" Jenny questioned. "I don't want to feel like this anymore. I feel useless and untrusted."

"I know how you feel, but I can't take you to somewhere he's not or would return to, and despite that, we can't change the past," William said.

"If he's not alive, where's his body?" Jenny investigated.

"It turned to dust along with the serpent, remember!" William replied.

"Why are you lying to me? Tell me the truth and give me back his book and the feather!" Jenny ordered.

"How did you know I had them?" William asked.

"I heard you say it out loud," Jenny replied.

"See, I told you to lower your voice," Rose said to William.

"Shut up!" William snapped.

"Well, William, now she knows, so what will we do? Give them back to her!" Rose retorted.

"No, I'm going to keep watch over these things he left behind because Jenny isn't mature enough to learn how to use them," William responded.

"Then teach me," Jenny requested. "He never taught me how to read his book or do anything he did. All I ever learned was that I had to see him fighting, and then I would try to imitate his moves. That's how I knew many of his techniques except a couple that he never showed in battle. I want to learn to make my style of moves and use them how I want them instead of using them as he does. William was my teacher; he taught me speed, power, and knowledge and taught me to fly as high as him, if not higher than he ever or will ever fly."

"That's what I wanted to hear, but it won't be easy," William said. "I'm not going to be soft on you like he was. You'll have to work harder than you ever had because my way of training is more rigorous and challenging. Even if he can't complete it, you can since Rose managed to."

"Of course I did," Rose said with pride. "And I'm twice as fast as he was."

"Well then, William, how strong are you compared to him?" Jenny asked.

"I really wouldn't compare myself to him. I would instead compare myself to my brother, who is on the council and stronger than Daemon; he wouldn't last 5 seconds against him," William responded.

"Well then, when do we start?" Jenny asked anxiously.

"In 1 month, I will only teach you if and only if you forget about him, and in exchange, I'll teach you how to use the feather to read his book and reveal what is hidden inside," William demanded.

Chapter 4: Another Prophecy?

It was six o'clock in the morning, and the sky was clear of clouds, and the sun shone brighter than usual. Its warmth was comfortable for the skin as if you were wrapped up in a warm sweater or inside a house, all cozy. The birds were out singing their layby. Jenny had been recovering for two days, and she still felt as if he were in the room with her, especially today.

"Today would have been our anniversary," she said. "Sadly, he's not here to celebrate it." She got on her toes and dressed. She then took his long black overcoat and hung it in the closet, hoping it wouldn't fall. She rushed out of her house and locked all the doors. All she had with herself was her cell phone, her white overcoat, his chain dangling from her snow-like neck, and his book, which William gave back for today, hoping she would keep her promise of not thinking about him and moving on with her life.

She met Rose near her home, and they walked

together down the streets full of people who just looked at them. On the corner of a street, they stopped, and as they turned, two people wearing overcoats were standing before them. One wore a long overcoat much like Daemon's that Jenny had. However, the man's overcoat was a faded grey that looked old and dirty and had stains that could have been a result of spilled blood only. The other person was a girl the same height as Jenny, wearing clothes similar to hers. However, this girl's eyes were hazel, and her hair was long and blonde. She appeared to be looking for someone, and the guy stayed quiet, blocking Jenny and Rose's path. The blonde girl approached them, stood before Jenny, and looked her in the eye. The man who accompanied her gestured for Rose to go with him, and she followed him to an alley.

"So, it's true," the blonde girl said.

Jenny looked at her, visibly confused, but slowly realized this person was not normal. Nothing about her was. Her eyes were hazel, but they were like a cat's. She studied the young girl intently, noticing she was holding something in her hands. Gradually, she realized that she was about to be on the receiving end of something. With a swift motion of her wrist, the mysterious girl ensnared Jenny by the neck with a long whip comprised of pieces sticking out of the edges like thorns.

"I don't know who you're talking about. I don't understand! Who do you think you are to threaten me like this?" Jenny asked.

"Stop playing stupid! You know exactly what I am!" the blonde girl roared.

"Who?! I don't know what you are talking about," Jenny replied.

"Stop playing games! Give it to me now before I snap that little neck of yours," the blonde girl responded, tightening her grip around Jenny's neck.

Jenny held on to the whip, trying to prevent the thorn-like ends from digging into her neck.

"Oh, we have a fighter here, don't we?" the blonde girl responded.

Jenny's eyes filled with tears. "What do you want?" she exclaimed.

"I'm starting to get annoyed. Why don't you just hand it over, and you could possibly live a few minutes longer?" the blonde girl suggested. "Look, darling, that is the only thing I came for. Everything else is disposable, so hand it over like a good girl!"

"I told you already, I don't know what you want!" Jenny said with a croaked voice.

"Let me explain myself then," the blonde girl responded. As she finished the sentence, her short hair suddenly turned deep purple and became long, reaching to her upper back.

"Now that's better," the girl said, giving Jenny a sharp look. "I hate using that form, but it's the only way to move about without alerting these specs of dust."

Jenny's eyes widened. "Wait... what are you?" she asked.

"I can't believe you haven't figured it out yet. You really are as stupid as the others say," the girl let out a sarcastic chuckle.

"Wait, what?!" Jenny said confusingly.

The girl licked her lips and said, "Name is Lilith. My master sent me here to look for something very important for him." She swiftly retracted her whip.

"What does that have to do with me?" Jenny asked.

"You are coming with me, princess," Lilith said in disgust.

Jenny looked at the girl's eyes and began to feel sleepy. Suddenly, a sense of helplessness took over her, like the sensation she had from it.

"What you are currently feeling is part of my abilities. You see, my curse gives me power over those weaker than me. I can subdue you by just looking at you. Honestly, you are such a weakling. I could have snapped your neck at any moment, but I must bring you alive. So be a good girl and go to sleep already!" Lilith exclaimed.

Lilith's eyes started changing into a deep dark blood-like color as her pupil slits were more pronounced. Jenny tried to look away but was eventually overtaken by them. She lost herself within the gaze of her new enemy, and her mind wandered. Slowly, Jenny heard a voice in the distance calling out to her. This voice was warm and familiar once again; his shadow appeared before her.

"What?" Jenny asked.

Jenny envisioned herself with Daemon; she could

see him as clear as day. Slowly, he began to talk to her, but something was off. She could feel it, but she didn't care. He was here, and that's all that mattered to her. Then something familiar happened. It was like a distant memory she thought she had forgotten. Her vision shifted into a lake, but it was all too familiar. She had been here before, and she knew it.

She thought to herself, *'It's all a dream; this isn't real!'* but just as she was about to wake herself up, something stopped her and teased her for her weakness.

"What a pathetic human you turned out to be," she heard in her imagination. Within her mind, she could see Lilith, but she was different. She didn't look like a person anymore. Before she was something else, she could see a pair of enormous bat-like wings, claws instead of hands, and bird-like feet with claws at the ends. Jenny felt her eyes looking deep into her soul.

The creature looked into her eyes and, slowly faded away and simply reappeared at her ears, speaking to her, "You are weak; stop resisting and come with me!"

Jenny, with tears in her eyes, was about to give in. Suddenly, she tried to call out for Rose, but noticed there was only the echo of her voice and nothing else. The creature mocked and laughs at her attempts. Jenny now tried to call William out, but the same situation occurred - only her voice echoed within the darkness.

Lilith simply stared at her, enjoying her desperation. "Yes, keep feeding me; feel it. You are useless! You are all alone, and no one is coming to help you!"

Right then, out of nowhere, a bright light covered the room with a feeling of safety and peace. As the light intensified, Lilith began to feel pain, and parts of her body slowly burned, and smoke came out. Jenny looked at what was happening and assumed Rose had figured out where she was, but the shadow within the light didn't resemble her. Rather, it resembled something else. Lilith cursed and, in pain, let out a piercing cry.

Then the figure vanished as Lillith herself turned to ash. She delivered one last warning before vanishing into thin air, "I will have you next time!"

The light faded, and an injured Jenny was found in an alley near where they first met the two figures. Rose picked her up, and as they made it to William's, she tended to her wounds.

"Don't move a lot. You're still all wrapped up in bandages. You were injured badly. It would help if you got some sleep, I'll come later to check on you. And please! Don't do anything all by yourself. If you need anything, call, and I'll come as soon as I can," Rose ordered her placing the phone off the table bed. "Don't worry, things will work out for the better soon. Just relax and take your time to feel better."

"You held your own. I'm impressed, or rather, I should consider you lucky since Lilith isn't the type to allow her to pray to get away so easily," William said.

"I don't want to talk about it…" Jenny said.

William asked Jenny to rest and relax and to allow them to take care of things. Later that night, William was looking over the agency's data on Lilith and other interests. The computer showed a photo of a young girl with blonde hair. The screen read as following:

Objective Name: Lilith, also known among her fellows as the mother of demons.

Appearance: Her appearance will usually take that of a young blonde woman in her early to mid-20s. When manifesting her abilities, her hair will turn purple, and her demonic origins will be more present as her hazel eyes will assume a different color and her pupils will change into slits like a cat's or a reptile's eye.

Abilities: Her abilities differ based on accounts; some sources depict her as using two or more abilities. The first of which is her usual ability known as a curse. Lilith's curse is known as 'Thorn,' which allows her to produce a whip or sometimes use her own nails as a 'Rose Whip' comprised of multiple thorns. Her second ability is only present in her second form (purple hair), which, like all demons, allows her to project images into others' minds. Her love for playing mind games on her victims results in severe trauma as she uses her opponent's own worries and insecurities against them. She is also capable of transforming into a human body, but since she considers all humans to be lower creatures, she chooses to use her own forms.

Lilith is also depicted as a predator and often attacks children and women. Her depiction is mainly of a human woman with both bird and snake-like attributes.

After going through the file and looking at the

images depicting Lilith, William continued going through his files as he stopped at Daemon's. The computer then shut off.

Jenny was on a bed, all wrapped up in bandages, unable to sleep since the day's incident. However, due to the anesthetic, she drifted off and fell asleep.

Chapter 5: Open

In the distance, two figures were fighting. The air blew as if the final battle was coming to an end. The two beings were covered in energy; one appeared white and pure energy, and the other appeared black and lifeless and seemed to rot even the very ground it touched. Both were engaged in a furious battle. The sky was black and red, and the sun was starting to set as neither side let up. The rain began to descend from the sky as all the living things in the ocean died and the oceans became bloody. Soon, the ground began to shake violently.

As time passed, it became dusk, and all that could be seen was a red moon with no love but blood, tears, and hate. In between the flashes of thunder and lightning, two figures could be seen. One a boy with long white hair and claws instead of hands. His skin was pale, his fangs were visible, and he was dressed in a long white overcoat, which was now mostly red because of all those he killed with his hands. His eyes were red and burned like fire as an awful scream erupted from him, shouting the name "Ezekiel!" He stretched out his arm, holding a sword as red as blood.

Meanwhile, another being of incredible purity stood nearby, radiating light like white flames that engulfed him and gave hope to those who had lost it. Both clashed as blood dripped from their wounds, but the white being began to sicken. He started to cry and coughed blood as the black being stared.

"That is why you're weaker than me. That illness of yours is what keeps you weak. You committed the crime and fell for a human. Not only that, but you got concerned for them! You must die!" the demon said. "You are the weak link in this world, and since you love humans so much, then I'll destroy you with them!"

"How ironic you say it, *brother* because you were the one who truly fell from grace, not me!" the white being snapped back. "I'm still here because I was entrusted with the mission to defeat you. It's like I said years ago. Ultimately, we all pay for our actions, sins, and decisions. As a whole, we are responsible for what happens. You should know this as well as I do because you were once one of us, an angel whose pride got the better of him."

"You know nothing," said the demon.

"Don't you understand you're a pawn? You'll be

thrown away just like I was! Once that happens, you'll know what I mean. Just look around. We are here, too, because we chose to fight! I learned that even we have free will and I am not the one to follow orders blindly!"

"Are you still with that? Don't you understand that no matter what you say, you can't change how I feel and see things? You are nothing more than my brother, but if you try to harm anyone, I will make you regret it! But, if you so much as touch one hair on her head or even leave a little scratch …. even the tiniest feeling that you have been close to her or tried to execute her, I will kill you with my own hands even if I go blind after or have to die! It will all be worth it after she is safe. I am free from…"

The television turned off abruptly. Jenny put down the remote and turned to her table bed and took her pills.

'And yet, I still can't forget about him,' she thought. *'What does Lilith want? And what is Lilith and her master after?'*

Jenny faced the ceiling and placed her hands on her face to try and understand what she was trying to do and why.

"She said they needed me for some reason. Daemon,

where are you? I need you here to explain to me what's going on," she let out her thoughts aloud.

Suddenly, the room grew cold as a draft of cold air opened the window in Jenny's room. A black feather fell gently inside the room, landing on the book on the table. Suddenly, she felt her hands moving on their own, reaching for the book. She picked the feather, placed the tip on her forehead, and said, "Please let this be a sign."

Then, she placed the feather on top of the book's cover, and the room brightened. The book's pages moved independently, turning on their own. She looked at the first page and began to see writing slowly appearing on one page. She began to look at the other pages, but only one page of writing was visible. Jenny grew frustrated as only one sentence showed, and even then, she couldn't read it. She threw the book across the room. The book landed open, and the pages turned back to the first page. Now, the words were visible, but she didn't understand the meaning behind them.

Chapter 6: The First Page

"Careful of what you seek, for what you seek may not be what you expected."

Jenny read the words as they appeared to her. She read the words about ten times to understand what the words on the page meant. And yet she was spellbound that no matter how she tried to find meaning, the only meaning she saw was "'It says careful for what you seek; for what you seek may not be what you expected it to be.' So does this mean that if I search for Daemon, it could be possible for him to have been dead for longer than one year, or maybe he only had a few hours to live then? Or someone impersonated him and his abilities, characteristics, and words?"

Jenny then had a flashback and saw a boy of white complexion who turned his body slightly behind to see her. His eyes were dark brown, and the look in them was of sadness and relief. "Sorry that I'm late, Jenny," he said.

"Daemon!" she said with a tear appearing in her eyes. "It's you! It's finally you... for a moment... for a moment, I thought you were…"

"No, I'm alive and stronger than ever," Daemon responded.

"They did everything they could, but neither matched him," Jenny said with tears rolling down her cheeks. She then looked behind her to see Wallace and Rose badly wounded and unconscious.

"I could feel them struggling as I made my way here," Daemon said as he got his overcoat and put it on her.

"Wait, Daemon, what are you doing?" Jenny said.

"I'm giving you my overcoat for protection. I know it's heavier than what you're used to, but it's thicker material and more resistant. Besides, it's long enough to keep a midget like you from getting hurt," he said, teasing her a little.

"So, this is it, isn't it?" Jenny said, looking at him with watery eyes.

"Yeah, it is," Daemon replied, keeping his left hand stretched and opening his palm to face his opponent while keeping the fire from reaching them. "Jenny, I'm genuinely sorry."

"Why are you apologizing? Wait, no, don't tell me you're going to…" Jenny asked.

"Jenny, don't make a scene. It's for the best," William said, struggling to get up while holding his right arm.

"William, take Rose and Jenny with you as far as you can, and don't let Jenny out of your sight for any reason, not even if it looks like I'm losing," Daemon ordered William.

"Yeah, like it usually looks like," William responded.

"Not even if she and Rose team up. It's an order: don't you dare let her out of your sight because if you do, and miraculously, I survive this fight, I'm coming after you, you got that?" Daemon commanded him again.

"I wouldn't have it any other way," William retorted. "Finally, you're acting like the leader. It was about time, so where were your leadership skills for the past years?"

William left and took Rose with him as Jenny spoke with Daemon one last time. She couldn't stop crying and finally said, "So is this it? Is this how it's going to end?

Why, you, Daemon, why must you always leave me behind?" she stopped and sighed for a moment. "I guess it can't be helped then, but Daemon, please promise that you will return to me safe and for good."

"Jenny, I promise," Daemon responded. "Don't worry. With my new power, I will win."

Everyone left while Daemon kept his attention on the serpent, and just as quickly, his eyes began to look like fire as if a living fire was alive and burning in his being. He looked directly at the snake and, with just a simple movement of his arm, put out the fire that the serpent was trying to use to finish everyone off.

"Long time no see," said Daemon.

"I would have wanted to finish those humans off. But you'll have to do so. You don't know how long I have waited to devour you, Daemon. I've longed to see the look of fear and desperation in your eyes and to hear you scream in terror like you did in your dreams," the voice said.

"I'm sorry, but I'm not here to fear you. You hold no power over me. Now, you're nothing more than an overgrown serpent with wings and feathers. You try to pass as my country's symbol, but you are nothing more than an abomination that I have feared for too long. I've grown. I'm not that little kid who used to fear looking at the sky and thinking that the moon was one of your eyes staring down at me, waiting for the chance to swallow me whole. Now, when I look at the sky, I see Jenny, and that's all the motivation I need to kill you," Daemon responded.

William turned around while carrying Rose and said, "Jenny, don't worry. You know Daemon better than that. He is tough, and you know it. I think he'll do the job just fine! It's his purpose, anyway."

"I know already," Jenny said, crying. "I know I must trust him and give him my support, but I can't believe he has to go."

"Hey, don't start getting emotional on me. I'm not Daemon. And yet, Daemon, you better come back," William said.

William, Rose and Jenny landed at an area where they saw a giant snake-like body moving and saw a small figure moving high in the sky, rising higher and higher. Suddenly, they saw a burst of white light coming from the small figure. The light slowly became intense and started to shine brighter than the sun. It was so bright that Jenny and everyone else went blind. Then, as the light began to fade, she saw the snake falling from the sky without moving.

"I don't see him," Jenny said worriedly.

William grabbed her arm and said, "Remember what Daemon said, Jenny."

"I know, but I'm still worried," Jenny said, denying his reassurance. "I must go to him. I want to see if he is still alive."

"Jenny, you must trust him. He'll win for sure!" William tried to convince her.

Jenny gave one last look at William, ran away from him, and approached the battlefield. William looked at Jenny while she ran away. He then looked at Rose and said, "That's how their love is. No matter what happens, they can't stay away from each other for long. And if I know them well, Jenny's reaction to going to Daemon shows how strong their love is. Daemon, now I see why you love her so much. She's pure, and her light is her own."

Jenny approached the battlefield to find Daemon crying blood and the snake badly burned.

'He can't go on much longer,' she thinks to herself. *'His illness is getting to him now; how I hate not being able to help him. Daemon's guard is up even though he has weakened the enemy.'*

Suddenly, the snake spoke. "I cannot believe it; you are not afraid of me! It's impossible! I am superior than you! I should be feared, especially by you! I will come back for you, and when I do, I'll devour that pathetic human you love so much, and then, I'll burn you alive where you stand," the snake said, spouting lies and fabricating threats.

Jenny watched from behind a tall building behind Daemon in horror. Daemon moved much slower as time passed, and his illness worsened. Now, he coughed blood. The snake saw Jenny hiding from behind, and as Daemon caught on to the idea, he moved with all his might and as fast as he could. He reached Jenny and carried her in his arms as he leaped out of the way of the flames.

"Why did you come? I told you not to," Daemon

asked.

"I had to make sure you were still alive and that you would keep your promise," she replied.

"You idiot! When have I broken a promise? Tell me," Daemon asked her.

"You never have," Jenny said.

"Then why must you talk like I've ever broken a promise?" Daemon questioned her once again.

The serpent looks at them and says, "How adorable your owner came to check on you, don't you see, Daemon, it's this filthy human. It's always them. They always break the laws, destroy what our master has created".

"Listen to yourself!" Daemon exclaimed. "You just called God our master when you proclaimed yourself a god ages ago."

"I have because our master won't destroy them," Snake responds. "He's too weak and sentimental towards his creations, especially these. I hate them, even the originals, but the girl was worth messing with such innocence and yet so foolish."

"So it was you who tempted Adam and Eve?" Jenny inquired.

"Of course, I was an angel, too, but not anymore," Snake replied. "Besides, Daemon fit his role well, and so did that other idiot."

"Shut up!" Daemon roared. "You used us to do your dirty work to take the fall. Now look at me. I'm ill, and this curse won't leave me alone."

Jenny watched as Daemon kept coughing blood. "Daemon, please let me help."

"No, you're no match for him. Besides, I want you to return with Wallace now," he replied.

"Daemon, please don't make me leave you, please don't!" Jenny pleaded.

"Jenny, I have to, or I'll never be able to finish this madness," Daemon said sadly.

The snake just watched and then said, "If you two can't seem to make up your minds, then I'll kill you both at once."

He took a deep breath, and a huge mess of flames burst from its mouth. As Daemon tried to protect Jenny, he created a light wall between him and Jenny, keeping her safe. Jenny desperately tried to break the wall to help Daemon, but the snake shot another blast of flames.

She saw Daemon smile, who said, "Don't worry, I'll always protect you even if I have to die in the process." As Daemon tried to block the attack, he got caught in it, and an explosion of the impact broke the barrier, sending Jenny flying about to crash into a skyscraper. Daemon suddenly appeared and held Jenny in his arms. As they were about to crash, Daemon enveloped Jenny in his arms and then closed his wings to protect them both. At the same time, his back faced the building. Then, they crashed and hit several walls until they hit the last 25 walls of the 1st floor of a 100-storey tall skyscraper. Once they hit the wall, they fell flat on it.

Daemon's black wings began to open up slowly. As they did, Daemon started coughing out and crying blood. Then, he loosened his embrace and saw Jenny safe and unharmed.

"Jenny, are you alright?" he asked.

"I'm okay. I wasn't hurt, but you didn't have to do that. You know I'm not a little kid; I can take care of myself," Jenny said.

"I'm sorry. If only I had taken the fight to another area, you wouldn't be stuck here with me," Daemon apologized.

"You don't have to apologize. It was my fault I returned even when you told me not to. We never seem to learn," Jenny remarked.

The snake then appeared wrapped around the building, broke through the ceiling of the last level, and began to release another burst of flames. As the flames came down, Daemon again embraced Jenny and closed his wings, keeping Jenny below him while his back faced the ceiling. His wings were closed around them to keep her out of the flames' reach. Daemon's back was badly burned, and smoke came out as if his back was being cooked.

Then, the snake tightened its coils around the building, sending it shuddering. As the dust faded, Daemon came out with a broken left arm, and Jenny appeared unharmed except for the few scratches on her face. Her pants were ripped from her legs, showing the white of her knees and part of her right leg. Dirt and tears streaked her face, and her makeup was smudged. She then saw Daemon rise into the sky with his wings spread. The snake also began to lift itself up into the sky.

Daemon then looked down at Jenny as he began to move toward the serpent, and in his mind, he thought, *Jenny, I'm sorry. I'm not going to complete my promise this once. I truly am sorry! I wanted to share more of our life, but my duty and my desire to protect you is keeping me away from you even more. Jenny, I'm sorry! I love you!'*

Daemon closed his eyes and took a deep breath. Suddenly, a blast of white light enveloped him; it was as white as snow. Then, a blast of energy released, sending Jenny flying far away. Once the light completely faded away, she faced the snake that had been burned to a crisp with its enormous yellow eyes staring back at her. Jenny let out a scream so loud it could be heard from the other part of the city. She then looked at the snake, which began to turn to dust as it faded away slowly. She searched for Daemon everywhere but couldn't find him.

"Daemon! You b****! Why did you promise me you would return if you're not here?" Jenny said, bawling her eyes out.

She then saw a black feather fall slowly from the sky as the gentle breeze of the wind carried it parallel to the moon. The feather fell slowly and dropped gently to the ground. As the feather fell to the ground, Jenny looked at it in astonishment. It burst into white flames that didn't burn anything, but a small black book appeared from the flames, and all those flames left was a patch of red roses that had never been there before. Jenny began to cry harder, looking at it.

As Jenny lay in her bed, she checked the clock to find that it was midnight and once again cried because of the harmful flashback. She took her pills, turned over, wrapped herself in the bed sheets, and fell asleep. From a distance, a shadow with wings watched Jenny as she fell asleep. Under the moonlight, it stood on top of a chapel.

A little kid of no less than five years old looked and said, "Mommie, look! I see an angel." The woman looked at the place the kid was pointing at but only saw the moon and carried on as if nothing had happened.

"But Mommie! I did see an angel! He was up there looking at that the window in that house!" the kid said pointing his finger at Jenny and Daemon's house.

As they walked away, the figure inside the room looked at Jenny and left a red rose on her bedside table. As Jenny turned her body to face the ceiling, the figure kissed Jenny on her lips and sneaked a feather in her hands. Jenny felt something soft and tightened her grip. Still, she only tightened her grip around the tip of the feather, leaving it intact. Just then, she whispered, "Daemon, where are you?"

The shadow looked at her for one last time and said, "Jenny, I'm here. I'm here right beside you. I do not promise this time, but I'll always try to protect you!"

Suddenly, Jenny opened her eyes and found no one in her room. "Strange, I could have sworn I heard Daemon's voice." And then, she saw the rose and the feather. "He was here," she said, looking out the window searching for him but only saw the moon. "I must have been dreaming."

High above, the figure was flying off, heading east to an unknown place.

"Jenny, I love you!" he said.

www.ingramcontent.com/pod-product-compliance
Lightning Source LLC
Chambersburg PA
CBHW051553120626
46551CB00013B/1496